QUESTION MARKS

"WHAT?"

written by
MICHAEL DAHL

illustrated by
CHRIS GARBUTT

Where do we find a question mark?

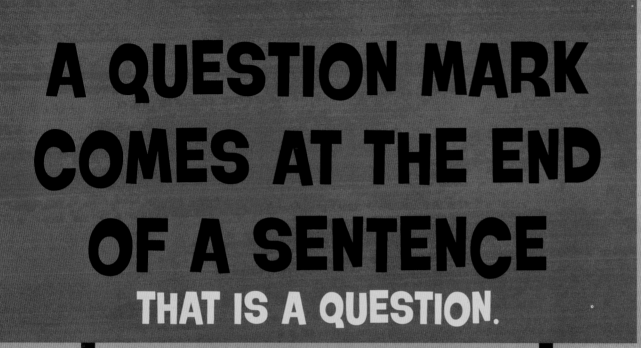

Questions often begin with WHO, WHAT, WHERE, WHEN or WHY.

WHO put all of these hats here?

WHAT does this mean?

WHERE is that hot-air balloon going?

WHY are all of the hats blue?

WHEN will these questions be answered?

We ask a question when we want to know WHO.

We ask a question when we want to know WHAT.

We ask a question when we want to know WHERE.

WHERE is that hat going?

We ask a question when we want to know WHEN.

HAPPY BLUE HAT DAY!
WHY were you riding in a hot-air balloon?
WHY were you leaving the crime scene?
WHY are you here?

ALL ABOUT THE

Question marks are found at the end of **SENTENCES THAT ASK QUESTIONS.**

Are you enjoying this book?

Can you help us find question marks?

Question marks help us get facts. They ask WHO, WHAT, WHEN, WHERE and WHY.

Who lost these hats?

Who is in that hot-air balloon?

What is that tiger doing?

What is behind that door?

QUESTION MARK

When will this mystery be solved?

When can we go home?

Where is the tiger going?

Where are you going?

Why weren't we invited to the party?

Why does this book have to end?

ABOUT THE AUTHOR

Michael Dahl is the author of more than 200 books for children and has won the AEP Distinguished Achievement Award three times for his non-fiction. He is the author of the bestselling *Bedtime for Batman* and *You're A Star, Wonder Woman!* picture books. He has written dozens of books of jokes, riddles and puns. He likes to play with words. At school, he read the dictionary for fun. Really. And his favourite words are adverbs (*really* is an adverb, by the way).

ABOUT THE ILLUSTRATOR

Chris Garbutt hails from a family of tea-drinking hedgehogs that live deep in the magical hills of Yorkshire. He has spent most of his time on this planet drawing cartoons and comics in London, Paris and, most recently, Los Angeles, where he now creates funny pictures in exchange for cake. Most recently he has been the executive producer, show-runner and art director of a TV series he co-created at Nickelodeon called *Pinky Malinky*, available on Netflix.

GLOSSARY

case a situation that is being investigated by the police

crime scene the place where something happened that was against the law

mystery something that is hard to explain or understand

question a sentence that asks something

replace to take the place of

solve to find the answer to a problem

Looking for definitions?

FIND OUT MORE

First Illustrated Grammar and Punctuation (Illustrated Dictionary), Jane Bingham (Usborne, 2019)

Oxford Primary Grammar and Punctuation Flashcards (OUP, 2015)

Visual Guide to Grammar and Punctuation: First Reference for Young Writers and Readers (DK, 2017)

COMPREHENSION QUESTIONS

1. What is a question that you would like an answer to?

2. We ask questions to learn about the world we live in. Name some jobs in which you would have to ask lots of questions.

3. What does a detective do? What kinds of questions would a detective ask?

WEBSITES AND APPS

Find some fun games for practising punctuation here:
www.funenglishgames.com/ grammargames/punctuation.html

Check out the **Squeebles Punctuation App** for fun activities to help you practise your skills!

OTHER TITLES IN THE SERIES

Commas Say "Take a Break"
Exclamation Marks Say "Wow!"
Full Stops Say "The End."

Raintree is an imprint of Capstone Global Library Limited, a company incorporated in England and Wales having its registered office at 264 Banbury Road, Oxford, OX2 7DY – Registered company number: 6695582

www.raintree.co.uk
myorders@raintree.co.uk

Text © Capstone Global Library Limited 2020

Editor: Shelly Lyons
Designers: Aruna Rangarajan and Hilary Wacholz
Creative Director: Nathan Gassman
Production Specialist: Katy LaVigne
The illustrations in this book were created digitally.
Printed and bound in India

ISBN 978 1 4747 7187 0

British Library Cataloguing in Publication Data:
A full catalogue record for this book is available from the British Library.